RAINFOREST
TREES AND PLANTS

Text and photography by Edward Parker

HODDER
Wayland

an imprint of Hodder Children's Books

© 2002 White-Thomson Publishing Ltd

Produced for Hodder Wayland by
White-Thomson Publishing Ltd
2/3 St. Andrew's Place
Lewes, East Sussex
BN7 1UP

Editor: Sarah Doughty
Design: Bernard Higton
Text consultant: Dr Paul Toyne

Published in Great Britain in 2002 by Hodder Wayland,
an imprint of Hodder Children's Books.

Produced in association with WWF-UK.
WWF-UK registered charity number 1081247.
A company limited by guarantee number 4016725.
Panda device © 1986 WWF ® WWF registered
trademark owner.

British Library Cataloguing in Publication Data
Parker, Edward
    Trees and plants. – (Rainforests)
    1. Rainforest plants
    I. Title
    581.7'34

ISBN 0 7502 3505 5

Printed in Hong Kong

Hodder Children's Books
A division of Hodder Headline Ltd
338 Euston Road, London NW1 3BH

CONTENTS

The rainforests are home to a huge variety of plants, ranging from giant trees to delicate orchids. This orchid is just one of thousands of species that thrive in the Amazon rainforest.

The interior of the Amazon rainforest in northern Brazil. Many large rainforest trees have adapted to grow in thin, tropical soils by developing special trunks to provide extra support.

THE VARIETY OF THE RAINFOREST

The word 'rainforest' conjures up all sorts of images: deadly crocodiles, giant snakes, agile monkeys, solitary jaguars, poisonous spiders and remote indigenous communities, all living within a hot and humid forest. All these exist only because of the fantastic array of plants, including trees, that make up the rainforest. Plants are the first link in the rainforest food chain. Without plants there would be no animals or people.

Rainforest plants come in an astonishing range of shapes and sizes. Some are giants, like the rattan which can have a stem longer than 150 m. Others are so tiny that their flowers are only visible through a magnifying glass. There are ancient trees, carnivorous (meat-eating) plants, plants that hitch rides on other plants, and plants that strangle their neighbours. Some plants are deadly poisonous, others have exploding seeds, and some tree species spend more than four months a year underwater. There are still thousands of rainforest plants that have never been studied.

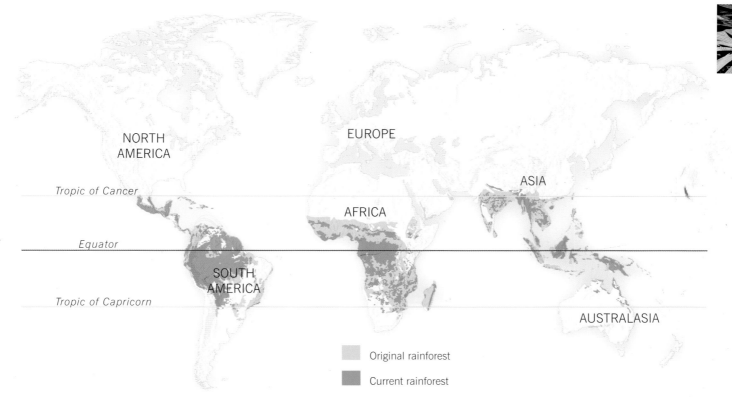

NORTH AMERICA

EUROPE

ASIA

Tropic of Cancer

AFRICA

Equator

SOUTH AMERICA

Tropic of Capricorn

AUSTRALASIA

Original rainforest

Current rainforest

Source: *World Conservation Monitoring Centre*

▲ *A map showing the extent of the world's tropical rainforests today, compared with their coverage 500 years ago, before large-scale deforestation began.*

WHERE ARE THE TROPICAL RAINFORESTS?

The tropical rainforests are found in a belt around the Equator, between the tropics of Cancer and Capricorn. In the tropics, temperatures are high and rainfall is greater than 2,000 mm every year. The largest area of continuous rainforest on earth is found in the Amazon region of South America. This area is similar in size to the USA, excluding Alaska. Rainforests are also found in Central America, Africa, South-east Asia and Australasia. This book will look mainly at the trees and plants of the Amazon rainforest.

TYPES OF RAINFOREST

Tropical rainforests can be divided into two main types, according to their height above sea level. These are lowland forest and tropical montane forest. Lowland forest contains some of the tallest trees and the richest plant communities in the world. The conditions in which they grow are hot and humid. There are about forty different kinds of lowland forests, including special types such as mangrove forest. Forests vary according to rainfall, types of soil and the drainage of the land. On higher ground, lowland forest gives way to the second type of forest, the cooler tropical montane forest. This occurs on hills and mountains above 900 m. Trees in tropical montane forests are typically much shorter than those in lowland forests. They are often hidden in dense mists, so are sometimes called 'cloud forests'.

▲ *An area of tropical montane forest in southern Colombia. The forest is cooler and shorter than lowland forest, and is home to many rare plants and animals.*

RAINFOREST SECRETS

THE TREE WITH A SNORKEL

Mangrove forest is one of the special kinds of lowland forest, and is found mainly along tropical coasts. The mangrove trees that grow in this habitat have developed special features that allow them to thrive in the salty, waterlogged conditions of their coastal environment. For example, mangrove trees have special 'breathing' roots that stick up out of the mud, like snorkels, and absorb oxygen directly from the air.

Mangrove forests are very important breeding areas for fish and birds. The shallow water beneath their bell-shaped roots provides a nursery area for juvenile fish, which keeps them safe from the large predators in the open sea.

▼ *The dense vegetation in the lowland Amazon rainforest is home to a huge diversity of plants, including climbing palms, vines and orchids.*

THE IMPORTANCE OF THE RAINFORESTS

Rainforests are important not only to all the animals and people that live in the forests, but to everyone on earth. Many important materials, such as rubber, come from rainforest trees. Many of today's medicines, such as quinine, also originated from rainforest plants. Today, scientists are continuing to study thousands of rainforest plant species in the search for more useful materials and medicines.

The rainforests are important for our planet because they help to maintain local and global weather patterns. Recent research has shown that the rainforests are absorbing around half of all the carbon dioxide sent into the atmosphere by human activities, for example in emissions from cars and factories. In this way, the rainforests are helping to reduce the effects of global warming.

2 PLANT DIVERSITY

◀ The giant Amazon waterlily is an aquatic plant that grows huge, circular leaves. The leaves are covered in sharp spines on their underside to stop aquatic animals from eating them.

Fascinating Fact

The largest leaf in the Amazon rainforest can grow to 2.5 m, which is bigger than the tallest basketball player.

PLANT LIFE

The world's rainforests are full of the most extraordinary variety of plant life. The Amazon alone is estimated to contain 80,000 flowering plants, which in turn support an estimated 30 million animal species, mainly insects. The rainforests of Africa, South-east Asia and South America are thought to contain as many as 180,000 species of plant. If this is the case, then nearly two-thirds of all the plant species that exist on earth occur on less than 7 per cent of the world's surface.

No one knows exactly how many species of plant there are today in the Amazon or in any other rainforest. Even the most well-informed scientists can only guess at the true diversity of plant life in these habitats. Unfortunately, it is unlikely that anyone will ever find out the true number of rainforest plant species, because every day more forest is being cut down, bulldozed or burned.

▼ This beautiful flower grows wild in the cloud forests of Colombia. It is also grown for sale as a decorative flower in the glasshouses of Europe and the USA.

GIGANTIC PLANTS

Many plants that have relatives in other parts of the world have reached gigantic proportions in the hothouse conditions of the rainforest. The giant Amazon waterlily, for example, has leaves that grow to over 2 m in diameter – large enough to float a small child on. Relatives of the modest fig bushes of the Middle East can grow to a massive size, and have a canopy more than 100 m in diameter. Other fig species can strangle the largest of rainforest trees, eventually causing them to die.

◀ *This giant araceae leaf is so large that local people often use it as a disposable umbrella.*

RAINFOREST SECRETS

INCREASING THE PLANT VARIETY

The activity of Amazonian Indians over thousands of years could have helped increase the number of plant species in the rainforest. Research in the Amazon has shown that much of the rainforest has been burned little by little over centuries. Indians have cut small gardens in the forest and then moved on every few years. Whenever the Indians moved they took useful plants with them for their new gardens. This gave the plants from another part of the forest new habitats in which to grow and evolve.

The existence of these gardens has been revealed by the burnt wood, pottery and other human remains found under the soil.

These former gardens, which are also known as black earth sites, have now been shown to have a greater diversity of plant species than the areas surrounding them.

UNIQUE SPECIES

Rainforests also contain thousands of plants that are not found anywhere else in the world. Far from being a chaotic tangle of vegetation, each plant species occupies a specific part of the rainforest. There is competition to survive and to reproduce, and this has forced tens of thousands of plants to evolve in ways that take advantage of particular rainforest conditions.

PLANT ADAPTATION

Many scientists think that the reason there are so many plant species in rainforests is that they have had to adapt to survive. Some plants, for example, contain substances that are poisonous to insects and so help the plant to survive.

▲ Thousands of species of plants are unique to the Amazon rainforest, such as this 'monkey chestnut' tree near Manaus, Brazil.

▼ This white orchid lives in the Madagascan rainforest and is pollinated by a single species of moth.

10

RAINFOREST SECRETS

THE HUMMINGBIRD AND THE HELICONIA

There are many different species of the brightly coloured heliconia plant in the rainforests of South and Central America. Each has large colourful flowers shaped like parrots' beaks to attract pollinators. The flowers of the different heliconia species allow only hummingbirds with bills of exactly the right length and curvature to reach the sugary nectar. When the hummingbird feeds, pollen from the flower sticks to the feathers on its face. As the bird moves from flower to flower, it pollinates other heliconia flowers.

Over time, new species of insect have evolved, which have become resistant to these poisons. This means that the plants have had to change in some way, or run the risk of becoming extinct. Furthermore, as plants often need insects to pollinate them, they must still attract those insects that are used for pollination, while repelling others.

An unusual feature of orchids is that many species are pollinated only by a single type of insect. The white orchid of Madagascar, for example, produces a large flower with an unusually long, thin tube. At the end of this tube is the nectar. The length of the tube prevents all insects from reaching the nectar except for a single species of moth, which has a tongue that is 450 mm long. The flower has evolved to allow only this species to pollinate it.

Fascinating Fact

There are estimated to be over 18,000 species of orchid in the rainforests of Central and South America.

3 THE RAINFOREST HABITAT

▲ *Every year, the large areas of forest that border the Amazon River become flooded, leaving only the tallest trees visible above the surface of the water.*

◄ *The lowland rainforest of the Amazon basin has fairly constant high humidity and warm temperatures, which provide ideal conditions for plant growth.*

RAINFORESTS OF THE WORLD

Tropical rainforests around the world look very similar from the air – but this hides the fact that each type of rainforest has hundreds of plant species that are unique to just that rainforest. Although a rainforest may look like a sea of almost identical trees, it is in fact a complicated jigsaw of many different plant communities. A single hectare of rainforest may contain over 300 different species of tree.

The world's lowland forests are the most widespread type of tropical rainforest, and they contain the richest variety of plant life in the world.

DIVISIONS IN THE FOREST

Variations occur because of the differing environmental conditions in which the plants grow. For example, an area of forest that is flooded every year has different types of plant from a rainforest that is found on higher, well-drained land. Equally, forests on high slopes are often very different from those on flat land. A particular division in the Amazon rainforest is made between forest that stands on land high enough to prevent flooding and forest that spends a part of every year either in or completely under the water. The higher, drier forests are known as the *terra firme* (dry land forest) while *várzea* is the term used for flooded forest.

RAINFOREST SECRETS

FLOATING GRASSES

The flooded forest of the upper Amazon is an extraordinary place, where the water level rises dramatically in the wet season. From March to August each year, the rains cause the river and its tributaries to flood, leaving only the tallest trees visible above the surface of the water. To cope with this flooding, many unique plants have evolved.

One plant is a thick-stemmed grass that grows on dry land for part of the year. As the floodwaters rise, it grows quickly to ensure that the top of the plant always remains just above the water's surface (see right). When the water becomes too deep, the plant detaches itself from the soil and joins with others to form vast floating rafts. When the water is at its highest, these rafts float away. Once the floods have receded, the grass puts down roots in another part of the forest.

RAINFOREST SECRETS

BUTTRESSES

The 'wings' of timber that spread out at the base of many rainforest trees are often called buttress roots. They are characteristic of hardwood trees that grow in the lowland forest. The buttress roots may spread up the tree trunk to a height of up to about 10 m.

The trees are able to grow to an enormous size while standing in poor, thin rainforest soils. Their buttressed shape helps them in several ways. Firstly, they give tall trees extra stability during violent tropical storms. Secondly, they provide the base from which the tree's lateral roots spread out under the ground, forming a shallow network.

NUTRIENTS FROM THE SOIL

The trees and plants of the Amazon rainforest grow mostly in poor, thin soils. And yet the Amazon rainforest is famous for its giant trees and luxuriant vegetation. This is because rainforest plants have evolved a way of using the nutrients needed to survive in poor soils. In most types of temperate forests, for example, more than 80 per cent of all nutrients needed by the plants are found in the soil. By contrast, in a rainforest, less than a quarter of the nutrients are in the soil. Over 75 per cent of the nutrients that are available exist in the living plants.

Fascinating Fact

Some tree species of the Amazon rainforest can spend more than four months of every year completely submerged underwater without any ill effects.

▼ *Although mangrove forests, such as this one in Queensland, Australia, contain fewer plant species per hectare than other types of rainforest, many of the species are unique.*

These nutrients are released when a plant dies and are quickly recycled and used in living organisms. Because the roots of rainforest trees are very shallow they can quickly absorb the nutrients of dead material broken down in the leaf litter on the forest floor.

▶ *(Above right) Mists can frequently be seen rising through rainforests. Rainforests control their own temperature to within a few degrees.*

LOCAL CLIMATE

Within a rainforest, the temperature and humidity remain fairly constant throughout the year, although there are extra-wet seasons in some forests. The forest protects itself from heavy rainfall with its canopy, and water runs quickly off its waxy leaves. Rainforests maintain the conditions that are ideal for growth. For example, plants control the temperature of the forest by evaporating water from their leaves, which cools the plant and gives rise to the mists that can be seen in the rainforests. This occurs within a rainforest even when the surrounding areas have been deforested and have a completely different climate.

THE LIFE CYCLE

In every type of rainforest, different plant species use many different strategies in their bid to survive and complete their life cycles. The tens of thousands of different plant species that make up each rainforest are alive today because their ancestors evolved methods of successfully completing the important stages of every plant's life – germination (sprouting), growth to maturity, the production of seeds and, finally, the dispersal of those seeds.

GERMINATION

Many rainforest plants start their lives in the gloom of the forest floor. Their seeds need sunlight to germinate. In mature forest, the canopy overhead blocks out most of this precious light. But when a tree is blown down, the light

▲ In areas where there is strong sunlight, or where a tree falls, many types of fast-growing trees and vines race to grow as high as the canopy and shade out their competitors.

Fascinating Fact

Pitcher plants often grow on the rainforest floor. Flies slide down the sides of these vase-shaped plants, and are trapped in the digestive liquid at the bottom.

briefly spills on to the forest floor, and the seedlings start a race against time and against each other. When a gap in the canopy has opened up, the young plants need to grow rapidly towards it, because in only a short time the canopy will be filled with leaves and branches once more. Some rainforest plants grow exceptionally quickly, but to maintain their rapid growth they have to make sure that not too many of their tender new leaves are eaten.

◀ In many types of rainforest there are vines hanging from the larger trees. Many of these vines protect themselves from being eaten by animals and insects by having poison in their leaves and bark.

GROWTH

Even when a plant has successfully germinated, it still struggles to survive. Thousands of different types of predator seek the precious resources and nutrients locked up inside the plant's living tissues. Leaf-eating caterpillars, wood-boring beetles, fungi and even mammals all eat plant material in order to survive.

EPIPHYTES

Not all plants start life on the forest floor. Many of the plants that do not grow from the floor of the forest belong to a large group of specialist plants called epiphytes. There are estimated to be 38,000 species of epiphyte, which include orchids, mosses, ferns, bromeliads and vines.

Epiphytes live in the canopy of rainforest trees. They grow on other plants without causing them any harm. A large rainforest tree may hold several tonnes of epiphytes in its branches. A single tree has been found to have 57 species of orchid growing on it, along with dozens of types of mosses and ferns. In Central and South America alone it is estimated that there are around 15,500 species of epiphyte that exist in tropical areas.

Fast-growing secropia trees have a very acidic sap, which deters wood-boring insects. They are also home to special ants that protect the trees from invading vegetation and plant-eating insects.

Many rainforest plants, such as climbing vines, use vicious spines and thorns to protect themselves from plant-eaters. These guard their fruits and seeds until they are ripe.

PLANT DEFENCES

Rainforest plants have developed an impressive array of defences to help them reach maturity. Tough leaves, thick bark, sharp spines and stinging hairs are all used for self-defence, to ensure that plants grow and survive. Some plants lure unsuspecting insects to their deaths by producing poisonous chemical substances. Others offer sugary rewards to ants for defending them. These 'ant trees' provide sugary food and special chambers for ant colonies. In return, the ants attack any insect on the tree, and help keep back other plants that might otherwise smother it.

CHEMICAL FACTORIES

Rainforest plants have used chemical means of defence for millions of years. Sustained by just sunlight, water and

LINKS

Plant defence and chewing-gum

Many rainforest trees and plants contain poisons or bitter-tasting chemicals to deter predators, while others ooze a sticky latex when their bark is damaged. This latex gums up the mouths of wood-boring insects. This process has been observed for centuries in the Amazon rainforest by the Amazonian Indians. They had already learned how to make use of latex long before the arrival of the European explorers in the fifteenth century.

In Central America, the Maya people chewed the latex from the sapote tree. Today, latex from this tree forms the basis of a multimillion-dollar chewing-gum and bubble-gum industry.

Fascinating Fact

The latex from the ballata tree in Guyana, South America, is used to make golf balls.

carbon dioxide from the atmosphere, plants are sophisticated chemical factories producing thousands of chemical compounds to help them survive. Some plants, for example, produce chemicals that are harmless whilst inside the leaf. However, when they are released from the leaf, the plant chemicals react with sunlight to form a deadly poison.

Other rainforest plants produce chemicals that affect the development of insect larvae. One group of chemicals, for example, prevents insects reaching maturity so that they cannot breed. Another group of chemicals makes an insect skip the stage of its life when it is a hungry leaf-eater.

◀ This Amazonian orchid has evolved a trumpet-shaped flower to only let in bees of exactly the right size to gain access to the nectar and to pollinate the flower.

▼ A flower attracts insects by its pattern and colour. Many insects see in ultraviolet light, which changes the flower's appearance when viewed by an insect.

SEED PRODUCTION

In order for any flowering plant to reproduce, it needs to produce seeds. A seed is produced when a pollen grain fertilizes an egg. This usually occurs when pollen is transferred from the stamen of one flower to the stigma of another flower of the same species.

Rainforest plants have developed ways of making sure that their flowers are pollinated – mainly by birds and insects. In the Amazon rainforest, the heliconia flowers that grow on the shaded forest floor are brightly coloured to attract birds. Some species of tree shed all their leaves to present thousands of strikingly coloured flowers in a spectacular show to encourage pollination.

INGENIOUS FLOWERS

Among the epiphytes, the orchids and bromeliads produce some of the most beautiful flowers and have evolved special ways of pollination. In some cases, the flowers have a narrow tube which has exactly the right dimensions for a single species of bee to gain access to the nectar and pollen.

▼ The structure of a flower. The top of the stamen is covered in pollen. Pollen from another flower is deposited in the stigma. This fertilizes the ovary at the base, so fruits can begin to develop.

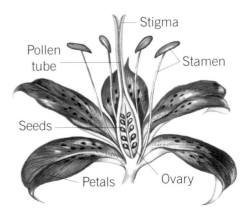

Pollen tube

Stigma

Stamen

Seeds

Petals

Ovary

RAINFOREST SECRETS

EUGLOSSINE BEES

Insects called euglossine bees live in the Amazon forest. These bees are vital to the lives of many types of orchid and trees. The bees and the orchids are an example of 'co-evolution'. This means that they develop together to the point where one cannot survive without the other. The bees, which pollinate Brazil nut trees (see right), cannot reproduce without a special type of orchid being present in the forest, and the same is true for the orchid, which also needs the bees for pollination (see below right). If the forest around a Brazil nut tree is cut down, the orchid disappears, followed by the bee, and the trees no longer produce nuts. As Brazil nuts are worth millions of dollars each year, the euglossine bees are also very important to the rainforest people.

Fascinating Fact

The world's largest flower belongs to the rafflesia. It grows up to one metre in diameter and smells of rotten meat to attract the flies that pollinate it.

Others have a petal that will only support an insect of the correct weight. Some, such as the vanilla orchid, have flowers that open at night. These flowers are usually white but have their own special scents to attract an insect or bat to pollinate them. Plants also use unpleasant scents to lure insects. Those plants that are pollinated by carrion beetles or flies often smell of rotting flesh, and their mottled flowers also look like decaying meat. Flies enter the flowers to lay their eggs in the 'pretend' corpse, and fall into traps where they are dusted with pollen before they can escape.

SEED DISPERSAL

In the life cycles of rainforest plants, seeds are produced. There is no guarantee that the seeds will be dropped in places where they can germinate and grow. These seeds have to be carried away from the adult plant and away from other seeds. Plants produce large numbers of seeds and spread them widely in the hope that they will land in a suitable place. Only a few species that flower in the highest parts of the rainforest canopy use wind to disperse their seeds. Plants such as the angelim tree have developed lightweight seeds with papery 'wings', which help them to float away easily in the wind. Some plants have developed seeds that have a corky layer so they can be carried away on rivers and ocean currents.

▲ The fruit of the catauari tree is eaten by tambaqui fish. The fish carry the seeds in their guts for several days before expelling them, thereby helping to disperse them.

◀ A collection of seeds on the forest floor, positioned for display. Some have papery 'wings' and are dispersed by the wind. Other seeds are inside fruits and are dispersed by being eaten.

FISH AND SEEDS

In the *várzea* (flooded forest) near Manaus, in Brazil, there are a number of trees which have special ways of dispersing their seeds.

In the wet season, the water level of Amazon and Negro Rivers rises by about 13 m, forming a very large lake. Many of the trees take advantage of their watery surroundings and produce fruits that fall into the water. The fruits are then eaten by fish swimming in the swollen rivers.

In this way their seeds are carried away by the fish to be dispersed in another part of the forest.

Fascinating Fact

Seeds can lie in the gut of large animals, such as elephants and tigers, for several days. During this time, the animals can travel very large distances.

NEW LIFE FROM SEEDS

Many of these seeds are dispersed by being carried or eaten by animals, birds and fish. Mammals such as agoutis, monkeys, deer, wild pigs, elephants, tigers and bats all transport seeds. To encourage animals to eat the seeds, delicious fruits grow around them. Once inside the stomach of an animal the fleshy fruit is digested, but the seed is protected by a tough outer wall and passes through the gut, usually without any ill effects to the animal.

Eventually, often many kilometres from the parent, the seed is expelled from the animal and starts life in a rich and organic environment.

5 PLANTS FOR PEOPLE

USES OF TREES AND PLANTS

More than 150 million people live in rainforests around the world, and many of them rely directly on rainforest trees and plants for their housing, food and medicine. Huge industries also rely on materials harvested from the rainforests. Tropical logs, for example, are turned into furniture, packaging, fax paper and barbecue charcoal, which is sold around the world. Rainforest plants also provide many of the raw materials for other important industries, such as those producing rubber, perfumes and chewing-gum.

Rainforest plants naturally produce an astounding array of chemical compounds. For many years, Amazonian Indians have been making use of plants which contain useful compounds to treat illnesses of various kinds. Western medicine has benefited from the rainforest plants and the knowledge of the Amazonian Indians to produce many drugs used in hospitals today.

▲ A man living in the rainforest in the African country of Cameroon uses raffia from a local rainforest palm to make himself a mat for sleeping on.

◄ Much of the world's timber and wood pulp used in industry comes from the rainforests of countries such as Indonesia, Guyana and the Ivory Coast.

Fascinating Fact

The fastest jets can only use tyres made from natural rubber. Alternatives are not able to withstand the extreme temperatures or stresses of landing.

PLANTS FOR RAINFOREST INDIANS

Amazonian Indians have a deep knowledge of the forest. They collect many types of material from rainforest plants, and also cultivate useful plants, such as cotton, in their gardens. The gardens generally include areas planted with manioc and fruit trees, as well as medicinal plants and palms that are used to build houses. The Kayapo Indians of Brazil use materials from around three-quarters of all the species of tree that grow in their forest.

LINKS

Annatto

Annatto (*Bixa orellana*) grows naturally throughout the rainforests of South and Central America. For thousands of years Amazonian Indians have used the waxy red substance that surrounds the seeds to make face paint. The Tsatchilla Indians of Ecuador (see right) use it to make a paste that they wear in their hair as an insect repellent.

Today, the red pigment extracted from the seeds is used widely as a safe natural colouring in food products such as margarine, yogurts, cheese and butter. In Europe, it has the label of E160b.

▲ A farmer stands with his crop of guarana fruit in the Atlantic forest of Brazil. In the future this may become a major world food.

▼ Brazil nuts are an example of a rainforest food from the Amazon, which is used in a wide range of foods – from muesli to ice creams and chocolate bars.

PLANTS AS FOOD

The Amazon and other rainforests have had a major impact on the food that is eaten by people all around the world. The banana plant, for example, was once restricted to certain areas of forest. Today, it is grown all over the tropics from the Caribbean Islands and Amazon rainforest to Africa, and is available in supermarkets to hundreds of millions of people. Other examples of rainforest plants with fruits that have become major world foods include cacao, pineapples, yams, avocados, breadfruits and coconuts. These are part of a global rainforest food economy worth billions of dollars each year.

Many other products that are important to the global economy are collected by local people from the rainforest. In the Amazon this includes thousands of tonnes of commercial nuts such as Brazil nuts, cashew nuts and macadamia nuts. Much of the work for rainforest people is seasonal, with millions of people working for just part of the year. Huge plantations have been set up for large-scale production of some foods, such as coffee.

FUTURE FOODS

Some of our future foods may well come from rainforest plants, especially those already used by local forest people. Palm fruits, such as acai and buriti, and other fruits, such as cupuacu, are already used to make vitamin-rich fruit juices and are popular flavours for ice cream. The brilliant-red fruits of the guarana plant are used to make fizzy drinks. There are also hundreds of species of legumes in the rainforest. These are related to commercial bean and pea plants, and may be used commercially in the future.

▲ A jackfruit sprouts directly from the trunk of the tree. Inside the fruit are a number of large seeds surrounded by sweet flesh.

RAINFOREST SECRETS

THE MYSTERY OF MANIOC

Manioc, or cassava, is a food used by millions of people. The starchy tuber is the staple food of traditional Amazonian Indians, and provides one third of the kilocalories eaten by African people. Manioc is, however, a mystery to botanists. The mystery is that the plant has only ever been found in the gardens of the Amazonian Indians, and never been found growing wild in the forest. Botanists are baffled because there are so many different types of cultivated manioc, yet there appear to be no wild relatives of the same species. In Amazonian Indian myth, manioc is explained as a gift from the moon.

NATURAL CHEMICALS

The natural chemicals that rainforest plants produce are used to defend themselves against attack. These range from simple sugars to the deadliest of chemicals. However, unlike industrial chemical factories, rainforest plants produce these compounds without polluting the environment, and by using the simplest of resources – water, sunlight and carbon dioxide.

Today, hundreds of the most effective drugs used in modern medicine come either directly or indirectly from chemicals taken from rainforest plants. For example, the rainforest has given us hydrocortisone medicines to treat conditions such as arthritis and rheumatic fever. Compounds known as alkaloids (which contain nitrogen) are gathered from the rainforest and have many uses in

▲ *Many rainforest communities make use of their expert knowledge of local medicinal plants. Western drugs are often too expensive for most people in developing countries, and local medicines are also found to be more effective against local diseases.*

medicine, for instance, as effective painkillers. There are many other famous examples of medicines that have been made from rainforest plants, such as quinine, curare and the anaesthetics that are based on cocaine.

FUTURE STUDY

Only a very few chemicals from rainforest plants have been studied compared to the huge numbers that exist. In fact, fewer than one per cent of plants have been screened for their medicinal usage. But several thousand species are believed to have anti-cancer properties. Many scientists believe that we are still only just beginning to find out about the natural medicines that can come from rainforest plants.

Fascinating Fact

The rosy periwinkle plant from the rainforest of Madagascar has a compound that has increased the chances of a child surviving leukaemia from 20 per cent to 80 per cent.

LINKS

Quinine

Quinine is a chemical that occurs naturally in the bark of the cinchona tree. It was discovered to be effective against malaria by the Amazonian Indians, and has been used for hundreds of years. In the nineteenth century, Europeans took both the plant and the traditional knowledge and produced quinine trees on a huge scale. Vast plantations in India and Java revolutionized the treatment of malaria around the world.

Today, around 100 million people are suffering from malaria. Surprisingly, despite all the advances of modern medicine, quinine is still one of the the most effective treatments for this disease. This baby (see below) is being given quinine. Quinine is also used as an antiseptic, an insect repellent and a sun cream.

◀ *The bark of some Amazonian trees gives off a bright-red dye. Some local people dye the fibres they use to make baskets.*

▲ *Wax from the Brazilian wax palm is used in many different products on sale throughout the world, including lipsticks.*

OTHER RAINFOREST PRODUCTS

Rainforest plants provide many other useful products in addition to food and medicine. A huge variety of natural plant materials occurs in the rainforests including oils, waxes and latex. Latex is very valuable and forms the basis of many industries, including the rubber and chewing-gum industries. Waxes such as that from the Brazilian wax palm are used for lipsticks. Natural dyes, aromatic oils and perfumes are also becoming increasingly important commercial products.

One of the most valuable products from the rainforest is commercial timber. Some timbers, such as mahogany, are very valuable. Others, despite their value to the environment, are considered to be of low value and are chipped and pulped and used to make paper, cardboard and chipboard.

▼ *This rubber tapper's house in the rainforest in Brazil is made entirely out of plant materials gathered from the forest.*

Aromatherapy Chemicals

On the Amazon island of Silves, village communities are cultivating rosewood trees in order to produce aromatic oils. These are used for aromatherapy in Europe and the Americas.

Aromatherapy is the treatment of an ailment by using the essential oils from plants. The strong-smelling oils are absorbed through the skin or inhaled, and are used for everything from antiseptics to anti-depressants.

Many of the essential oils used in aromatherapy come from rainforest plants.

The plants used include the ylang-ylang, sandalwood and rosewood trees. However, other rainforest plant oils also have strong aromas that could be used.

Fascinating Fact

Hammocks made from cotton or other plant fibres from the rainforest are popular places to sleep as they are much cooler than traditional beds.

Millions of rainforest people continue to build their homes from rainforest plants. These include rot-resistant timbers and strips of bark. Some homes may have walls made from split palm stems, such as the chonta palm used by the Waorani Indians in Ecuador, or thatch made from palm leaves. Rainforest timbers are used extensively around the world in construction as well as palm trees and bamboo. In Asia, bamboo from the tropical forests is used not only as a building material, but for scaffolding needed in the construction of modern buildings.

Rainforest people often use rainforest products to furnish their homes. Products such as baskets, mats and sieves are made from vines, leaves and canes and from fibres stripped from palms.

THE LOSS OF TREES AND PLANTS

It is estimated by the World Conservation Monitoring Centre that 400,000 hectares of Amazon rainforest are being cut down each year. This is the result of activities such as mining, logging, road building and clearance for agriculture. Also, the rate at which the rainforest trees are now disappearing, especially in the Amazon, is now speeding up. No one knows exactly how many plant species are becoming extinct, but it could be hundreds every year. Many other plants are becoming very rare.

The loss of rainforest trees changes the habitat for the other plants that live in the rainforest. Once the canopy has disappeared, many plants that grow on the ground cannot survive. The soil is exposed to the hot tropical sun and heavy rains, and is no longer able to support all the plants that once grew there. Colonizing plants invade these areas, smothering any plants that remain on the rainforest floor.

▲ A scene from the state of Acre in the Amazon rainforest, where the forest has been burned down and local cattle ranchers have moved cattle in to feed on the new plant shoots.

Fascinating Fact

In Cameroon, the bark of a type of small tree was found to help cancer. Many trees were cut down and the bark sold – the tree is now very rare.

LINKS

Soya Beans

Soya beans are a very important worldwide crop. Soya is used in a wide range of processed human and animal foods. However, cultivating soya beans is causing great damage to the Amazon rainforest. Large areas are burned every year (see right) to make more land available for soya beans. The land is managed by the 'soya kings'. They are paid subsidies for using the land for soya and have the support of big companies. The 'soya kings' are planning to increase the area under soya cultivation to 10 million hectares in Brazil.

Some rainforest trees, such as mahogany and secropia, do recover and grow quickly but it could be hundreds of years before the forest recovers completely.

▼ An area of steep rainforest land in Madagascar which has been cut down to make way for a small forest garden.

CASH CROPS AND CATTLE

Rainforest plants are destroyed every time the forest is cut down to make way for new agricultural land. Often the sorts of trees that are bulldozed and burned are very valuable species. The planting of cash crops, including oil palm in Indonesia, tea in Australia and soya beans in Brazil, has caused large areas of rainforest to disappear. Cattle ranching, especially in the Amazon rainforest and Central America, has also caused huge areas of forest to be destroyed.

◀ In the north-east of Brazil, hundreds of thousands of people are searching for small areas of land on which to grow food. Many enter the Atlantic rainforest and cut down the trees to clear a plot for agriculture.

▼ Large commercial ventures, such as the setting up of oil palm plantations in Cameroon, Indonesia and Ecuador, can lead to the destruction of large areas of rainforest.

LANDLESS PEOPLE AND THE DISAPPEARING FOREST

Today, large areas of rainforest land have been replaced by farmland. Often the areas that make the best farmland are owned by a few powerful people who control the use of the land. But poor people also enter the forest to cut down the trees and plants in an effort to farm the land and support their families. In the rush to grow food to eat, they are destroying many types of rainforest plant.

This has happened in Brazil. Its Atlantic rainforest once formed an almost unbroken forest along the Atlantic coast. Today, only 5 per cent of this magnificent forest remains. The state of Bahia contains one of the largest areas of the Atlantic forest – much of it owned by only a handful of families. In 2000, about 250,000 landless workers in Bahia tried to occupy land in the forest in an attempt to grow food to feed their families.

LINKS

'Advance Brazil'

In an attempt to become more like 'developed' countries, the Brazilian government has announced a plan to cut down and develop large areas of the Amazon. In a scheme called 'Advance Brazil' the Brazilian government is planning to spend US $40 billion over the next twenty years on roads (see right), hydroelectric power schemes, river channelling and gas pipelines. Its goal is to expand logging, mining and agricultural industries across the Amazon. If this plan goes ahead deforestation will rise to more than 500,000 sq km per year by 2020 and many rare plants will become extinct.

In many parts of the world, this rainforest settlement has been encouraged. Huge numbers of poor people have been moved by governments from overcrowded cities to rainforest areas to start new lives.

THE ROAD TO RUIN

In rainforests like the Amazon, the rivers have always been the highways. Today, new roads are created by logging companies or by government schemes providing routes into a new area of forest. Soon after a road has been created, landless people can be seen moving along it on their way to claim areas of forest, which are then cut and burned. This has accidentally introduced non-rainforest plants into fragile areas, which can change the local plant ecology and could cause some plants to become extinct.

LOGGING

The world's rainforests are rapidly losing their wealth of plants due to logging and the timber industry. Often logging companies harvest the most valuable timber without thinking about the future of the rainforests or the people who depend on them. Huge areas may be 'clear-felled' leaving just stumps, brushwood and bare earth. In a matter of a few weeks a rainforest that has taken thousands, even millions, of years to evolve will have been turned into a worthless desert.

Logging not only causes destruction in the harvested areas. It also upsets the fragile balance of ecology in the forests around the cut areas. To make things worse, once the cover of trees has been removed, the heavy tropical rains wash away the thin soils. This makes it very difficult for the rainforest plants to recover.

▲ Logging is having a major impact on rainforests around the world. Millions of tonnes of timber are logged every year. Much of this timber ends up as paper and packaging, in countries such as Japan and the USA.

WOOD FOR FUEL

For millions of people around the world, the wood that comes from the rainforest is their main source of energy. Even in Nigeria, a country rich in oil, more than 80 per cent of the population relies on fuel from wood – often in the

form of charcoal made from rainforest trees. Because of the rising numbers of people who live in or near to rainforests, charcoal use is having a serious effect on rainforest plants. The manufacture of charcoal can stop areas of rainforest growing back, because young trees are just as suitable for charcoal as mature ones.

◄ In countries such as Tanzania, charcoal is the main source of fuel for millions of people. With such a huge population, the rainforests will continue to suffer due to charcoal burning.

RAINFOREST SECRETS

MANGROVE DISAPPEARANCE

The mangrove trees that grow along tropical coasts have now been reduced to around 14 per cent of the area they once covered. This has been caused mainly by people cutting wood for fires (see right), and pollution has also played a part. The main threat, however, has come from shrimp farms. Shrimps are very valuable to many countries as an export. Shrimp farmers clear the mangrove forests, which are breeding grounds and nurseries for many commercial species of fish. This reduces the number of fish in the area and is a loss for local commercial fish farmers. If the area silts up, the shrimp farmers move to a new shrimping ground. The silted area that was once rich forest is likely never to recover.

HELPING THE RAINFORESTS

Many individuals and environmental organizations are trying to find ways to help conserve tropical rainforests and the plants that grow in them. Their work includes setting up protected areas, and supporting the rights of traditional rainforest people. They are also encouraging renewable resources – such as Brazil nuts – to be harvested.

In the world's wealthier nations, some people are helping to save rainforests by using fewer forest resources. They try to use more items made from recycled material, or to buy only from properly managed forests. They also try to make other people aware of the effects of destroying the rainforests.

Logging on a large scale is usually the result of action by governments, large businesses and international organizations. If the rainforests are to be protected, the attitudes of these groups need to change. Pressure from environmental groups means that this is already happening. In the future, it may benefit those who make decisions about rainforests not to cut them down. There may be money available to encourage people to conserve it.

◀ This man is collecting rubber in the Chico Mendes Extractive Reserve in the State of Acre, Brazil. Collecting rubber in this way provides employment for local people, and does not lead to the forest being destroyed.

▼ A young East African boy who lives close to the Udzungwa Mountain Forest National Park in Tanzania. He is about to plant these small trees in the forest.

RAINFOREST SECRETS

'GREEN' CHARCOAL

Along the edge of one of the largest remaining areas of rainforest in Tanzania, local schools are working on a plan of action to help reduce the amount of wood for fuel that is taken from the rainforest. Local teachers have not only set up tree nurseries for replanting the forest, but have also found a way of making a new fuel that does not need timber from the forest. Using a mixture of dried leaves, wood ash, sand and water (see far right) it is possible to make a fuel which burns very much like charcoal (see right).

SUPPORTING INDIGENOUS PEOPLE

For tens of thousands of years, indigenous people have been carefully looking after the rainforests. Indigenous people believe that plants, animals and people should all share the forest. Areas of forest where Amazonian Indians have lived for thousands of years contain a huge variety of plants because the Indians themselves have increased the diversity. It is only when Indians are pushed out of their land and outsiders arrive that the forest and its plants are in danger of being destroyed. Allowing indigenous people to live in certain areas of rainforest, free from the activities of outsiders, is one way of protecting the forest and the many plant species that live within it.

SAVING THE RAINFORESTS

People can help to save the rainforests by using alternatives to rainforest resources. For example, instead of using rainforest trees as a source of timber, rich countries could recycle wood or buy plantation timber.

People could also reduce the need for the huge soya plantations planned for the Amazon rainforest by making a choice to eat less meat and processed foods from soya-fed animals. Alternatively, they can ensure that their food is from animals that have been fed soya from 'certified' sources, where no trees were cut down to grow the soya.

Rainforests are also affected by pollution and will suffer from the effects of global warming. Most industrial pollutants, especially greenhouse gases, come from the wealthiest parts of the world, such as North America and Europe. Individuals and governments could help the rainforests of the world by reducing pollution.

▲ In the Colombian cloud forest reserve at La Planada, children visit the area to learn more about the nature of the forest, and to gain an appreciation of the rainforest habitat.

LINKS

Eco-labelling

It is not always clear where wood products come from. The idea behind eco-labelling is to let people see where a product comes from, so they know whether or not it has come from a well-managed forest.

One of the most successful schemes is organized by the Forest Stewardship Council (FSC). The FSC provides a way of checking where the timber has come from and how it has been harvested. The FSC logo is a stamp of approval given to well-managed forests all over the world.

Any product carrying its mark guarantees that it does not come from the sort of logging that is destroying the Amazon rainforest, and ensures that the rights of rainforest people are being respected.

▲ In the community of Novek in southern Mexico, a forester checks how well replanted rainforest trees are growing.

ENVIRONMENTAL GROUPS

Environmental groups make people aware of the issues concerning rainforests. Many have tried to get governments and international organizations to think again about how rainforests are managed.

Some environmental groups such as WWF, Friends of the Earth and Greenpeace have been successful in making governments make changes in the law to protect the rainforests. Some of these groups have also helped to protect the rights of rainforest peoples to the land they live on. Small groups, known as Non-Governmental Organizations (NGOs) have also been involved in practical rainforest conservation projects. Many of these projects are organized by local communities.

◀ Udzungwa Mountain forest is one of the last remaining large areas of tropical montane forest in East Africa. It has been protected by both its status as a National Park and by local community culture, which allows people to collect only fallen wood, and prohibits any logging.

▼ A researcher's notes and a flower collected as part of a survey on medicinal plants in a montane forest area of Ecuador in South America.

PROTECTED AREAS

It is not often that an area of rainforest is protected to help rare types of plant. However, in some countries it is now illegal to cut down certain types of rare trees or collect other rare plants such as orchids. Usually the best way of protecting rainforest plants is by making an area of forest into a park or reserve.

At present, only a small part of the world's remaining rainforests have any legal protection. Environmental groups such as WWF and Friends of the Earth are trying to help save the rainforests by campaigning for their urgent protection. WWF's Forest for Life Campaign, for example, has set a target that each country should have a network of protected areas that contains at least 10 per cent of each type of forest. While this has been a very successful campaign, some of the countries with the largest remaining areas of rainforest have not yet met this 10 per cent target.

RAINFOREST SECRETS

'DINOSAUR' PLANTS

The forest of the Special Reserve of Anjanaharibe-sud is in Madagascar. In 1998, a local forest officer was walking through a part of the forest. He spotted an unusual plant which turned out to be one of the rarest plants in the world.

Only seen once before, in 1909, the taktajania plant (see right) dates back over 250 million years to a time when Africa, Madagascar and South America were all joined together. It is unlike any existing plant and its nearest relative is thousands of kilometres away. Finding the taktajania plant was one of the most important botanical discoveries of the twentieth century – a real 'dinosaur' tree.

▼ Rare orchids being bred and studied at the Royal Botanic Gardens at Kew, in London.

Nevertheless, vast areas of the Amazon rainforest in Peru and Colombia are now protected as a result of this action.

SEED BANKS

One of the ways of conserving rainforests is by the setting up of seed banks. Seeds are collected from rainforests from all around the world and kept in huge refrigerated storehouses. The seeds of tens of thousands of rainforest plants can be stored at one seed bank. One of the largest seed banks is at the Royal Botanic Gardens at Kew, in London where it is hoped that eventually the seeds of 10 per cent of the world's plants will be kept.

43

THE FUTURE

The future of the world's magnificent rainforests and the plants that live in them now hangs in the balance. We are still losing rainforests at an increasing rate. In the case of Brazil, the plan to 'Advance Brazil' will destroy vast areas of the Amazon rainforest and greatly reduce the diversity of plant life on earth. The planned roads, soya plantations and oil and gas pipelines will change the landscape forever. However, the scheme faces a lot of opposition. There is a great deal of interest in the rainforests today, and an awareness about the loss of the forest trees and plants, which places pressure on industry and governments.

PROTECTION FOR RAINFORESTS

There are some governments, large companies and individuals around the world that are making huge efforts to save the rainforests alongside environmental groups such

▲ *The silhouettes of Brazil nut trees against a sunset in the Amazon rainforest. These trees no longer produce nuts because the rainforest around them has been cut down, and the bee that pollinates them no longer exists here.*

▲ A scientist working with WWF in Madagascar stands next to the sign of a National Park near the town of Andapa.

as WWF and Greenpeace. Schoolchildren living in or near the rainforest are becoming active in protecting and replanting the forest for their future, and many other children are also campaigning to save the forests, so these habitats will still exist when they grow up. People now have the choice to buy products that come from well-managed areas of rainforest and refuse to buy products made from rare plant material. The actions taken in the next decade will decide the fate of a vast amount of the world's rainforest, and the fate of the precious trees and plants that live in them.

RAINFOREST SECRETS

THE INHERITORS OF THE PLANET

In an area of tropical montane forest around a lake called La Cocha in southern Colombia there is a group of remarkable conservationists. Ranging from the age of four years upwards, about one hundred young people such as this girl (see right) are part of an environmental network called 'Inheritors of the Planet'. Around La Cocha, on the small farms where they live, they have been organizing tree nurseries, replanting areas of montane forest, and campaigning for the forest to be protected and used in a sustainable way.

In February 2001, the president of Colombia acknowledged the work of the group by making the area 'A gift to the earth'. This will protect the area from future development projects and so ensure its long-term future.

GLOSSARY

A heliconia flower from the rainforest.

bromeliads A group of plants that originate in the Americas and have a rosette of spiny leaves.

buttress The name for the roots that grow from the trunk of a tree above ground and help to support it.

canopy The layer of trees between the forest floor and the tallest towering treetops.

cash crops Products such as cotton and sugar, which are sold as a way of earning an income.

conservation The maintenance of environmental quality and resources.

ecology The study of the inter-relationship between organisms and all aspects of their environment.

epiphytes Plants that grow on other plants.

extinct When the species of any living organism, such as an animal, a tree or a plant no longer exists.

germination The beginning of the growth of a seed into a plant.

global warming The gradual increase in the temperature of the Earth's surface, caused by high levels of carbon dioxide in the atmosphere.

habitat The natural home of a particular plant or animal.

humid Usually refers to when weather conditions are warm and damp.

indigenous Belonging originally or naturally to a particular place.

larva The stage between the egg and the pupa of insects such as caterpillars, maggots and grubs.

legumes Soft, dry fruits that are held in a pod, such as peas and beans.

mangrove A swamp forest found on tropical and sub-tropical tidal mud flats.

nectar The sugary substance produced by plants and made into honey by bees.

nutrients Any substances that provide essential nourishment for living organisms.

plantation timber Wood from trees grown in purpose-made forests, which are called plantations.

pollinate When pollen is transferred from the male to the female parts of a flower.

predators Animals that naturally prey on other animals.

ranching Farming that is primarily involved in cattle-breeding and rearing for meat.

renewable resources Products such as fruit, nuts and fish, which can be harvested regularly and will naturally make up their numbers.

reserves Areas of land that are protected, usually because of the plants or animals they contain.

sap The vital liquid that circulates inside plants.

savannah Open grassland in tropical or subtropical areas where few trees or bushes grow.

species A group of plants or animals that closely resemble one another.

stamen The male fertilizing organ of a plant.

stigma The female part of a flower that receives the pollen during pollination.

subsidies Financial assistance given to organizations to support them.

ultraviolet light (UV) Part of the light spectrum that can be seen by certain types of insects.

FURTHER INFORMATION

BOOKS TO READ

The Amazon Rainforest and its People by Marion Morrison (Hodder Wayland, 1993)

Antonio's Rainforest by Anna Lewington (Hodder Wayland, 1998)

Closer Look at the Rainforest by Selina Wood (Franklin Watts, 1996)

Geography Detective: Rainforest by Philip Sauvain (Zöe Books, 1996)

Journey into the Rainforest by Tim Knight (Oxford University Press, 2001)

Jungle by Theresa Greenaway (Dorling Kindersley, 1994)

The Rainforest by Karen Liptak (Biosphere Press, 1993)

Secrets of the Rainforest by Michael Chinery (Cherrytree, 2001)

The Wayland Atlas of Rainforests by Anna Lewington (Hodder Wayland, 1996)

WEBSITES

There are many websites about the rainforests. Type in key words to search for the information you need, or visit the following sites:

Passport to the Rainforest
http://www.passporttoknowledge.com/rainforest/main.html
Includes map, graphics, images and information about plants and animals.

Rainforest Action Network
http://www.ran.org/
Facts about rainforest people and animals presented in a question and answer format. Includes action that children can take to conserve the rainforests.

Rainforest Conservation Fund
http://www.conservacion.org/
Provides species data for plants and animals. Also includes news, projects and articles.

Rainforest Information Centre
http://www.forests.org/ric/
News, information, ecology and conservation. Includes a links page for children.

Species Survival Network CITES Conference
http://www.defenders.org/cites.html
Information on CITES conferences, which discuss the world's endangered species. It includes appendixes of endangered animals and plants.

World Rainforest Movement
http://www.wrm.org.uy/
Includes information on rainforests by country and by subject.

WWF–UK
http://www.wwf-uk.org/
In addition to its main website in the UK, the environmental organization has a number of sites devoted to different campaigns.
http://www.panda.org/
The international site for WWF.
http://www.panda.org/forest4life
The forests for life campaign.

Visit learn.co.uk for more resources

VIDEO

The Decade of Destruction by Adrian Cowell (Central Independent Television, 1991)

ADDRESSES OF ORGANIZATIONS

Friends of the Earth, 26-28 Underwood Street, London N1 7JQ Tel: 0207 490 1555
http://www.foe.co.uk/
Greenpeace, Canonbury Villas, London N1 2PN Tel: 020 7865 8100
http://www.greenpeace.org.uk/
Oxfam, Oxfam House, Banbury Road, Oxford, OX2 7DZ Tel: 01865 312610
http://www.oxfam.org.uk/
Survival International, 6 Charterhouse Buildings, London EC1M 7ET Tel: 0207 687 8700
http://www.survival-international.org/
WWF–UK, Panda House, Weyside Park, Godalming, Surrey GU7 1XR Tel: 01483 426444
http://www.wwf-uk.org/

INDEX

Picture acknowledgements:
All photographs are by Edward Parker with the exception of the following: Chapel Studios 19 (Zul Mukhida), NHPA (cover), Still Pictures (Mark Edwards) 29. Artwork is by Peter Bull.